EMBODYING MY I AM

EMBODYING MY I AM

Affirmations and Notes of Comfort

KISHNA MARIE

Kae-oh Publishing

Copyright © 2022 by Kishna Marie

All rights reserved. No part of this publication may be reproduced, stored, or transmitted in any form or by any means, electronic, mechanical, photocopying, recording, scanning, or otherwise without written permission from the publisher. It is illegal to copy this book, post it to a website, or distribute it by any other means without permission.
Kishna Marie asserts the moral right to be identified as the author of this work.

Paperback ISBN: 978-1-7372797-8-5
Hardcover ISBN: 978-1-7372797-2-3

Printed and Bound in the United States
First Printing, 2022

Introduction

Kishna *Marie* at an early age found power in writing, and with that power, she would journal to deal with the trauma and pain that encircled her. She would often write about "how her beauty rose out of her pain". Then one day as she was journaling, she realized that her beauty was not in the pain she endured and was overcoming, she remembered that her beauty is in her being, and her being is a part of the great *I AM*. Kishna *Marie* remembered who she was, whose she was, the bloodline she came from...and started writing affirmations and notes to herself in her journal. She would go on to draft beautiful stories about where her life was headed and what she deserved. The journaling was healing and gave Kishna the power to live in her purpose and just be.

In this book, Kishna shares affirmations and notes of comfort that she used as healing agents early on in her journey of healing.

To Timmy, always remember, that you are the light and *I AM* as you are one of many.

*My heart is filled with joy because I **tripped**,
I fell,
I rose,
I rested,
I rose back up moving freely letting my mind and heart guide my body not caring about how I look, just caring about how I feel.
It feels good to move at my own pace even going to the edge but having the knowledge that I am not ready
or
in the right moment ready to jump.
I just keep moving under the*

guidance and awareness of spirit.

*I fill my mind,
body,
and heart
with small doses of words that
heal
my soul.*

*I had to seek refuge in myself and find the answers I was looking for.
In looking for the answers I found myself.
I was capable of being a woman of more by living out what I scribbled in my journals as a little girl, the answers that already resided in me, the answers that would not let me settle until I found them again.*

*I found those answers within me...
in a room full of chaos...
while I was alone.*

I am supported by the universe.
My soul is free.
My body is energized.
My mind is clear.
My heart is smiling.

*Faith is knowing that all valleys have peaks and all peaks have valleys.
In understanding that I will be
patiently waiting,
graciously preparing.*

*The
releasing
of
attachments
made room for me to root,
heal,
and
grow.*

*I found peace where there once was darkness in me.
I sat in my darkness with patience, forgiveness, and compassion
honoring it,
dismissing it,
and welcoming in the light
as it
overshadowed
the
darkness.*

*I wake every morning
possessing a renewed and
invigorating energy that I
prayed for the night before.
I pray this energy carries me
throughout the day and night
activating
the acts of empathy,
patience,
comfort,
confidence,
determination,
and awareness when needed.*

*Once I surrendered to the
natural state of who
my source,
my guiding light
said
I am...*

I flourished.

*Remedying what was and
remembering to always be me.*

I surrender my mind,
body,
and
heart
to resting
in
the stillness that my
soul
has been craving.

*Honoring and respecting
where
I am at
right now
mentally, spiritually, and
physically
enables my growth and allows
me the flexibility in my
journey
to pause,
stop,
and rest.*

*I slow down,
stop,
and
listen to my body.
In slowing down and stopping
I honor the support system of
my mind, body, soul, and heart.
That support system takes care
of my vessel so my vessel can
take care of its support system.
They work together
strengthening each other and
themselves commissioning me to
become a beautiful masterpiece.*

*The calmness of my mind and
the stillness of my body allow
my spirit to be at rest
permitting me to secure
a safe space
within
myself to feel and understand
my emotions safely.*

I am a living being in whom
HE
breathed
life
Into.

I am paying attention to my breath for it is what gives me life.
My breath connects every fiber in me, relaxing me from the top of my head to the tips of my toes enabling me to feel every pulsation flowing through me.
I am relaxed in stillness honoring my breath remembering that breath is a sacred gift that fills me with Life.

Breathe in for five seconds
1, 2, 3, 4, 5
Breathe out for five seconds
5, 4, 3, 2, 1
Breathe in for five seconds
1, 2, 3, 4, 5
Breathe out for five seconds
5, 4, 3, 2, 1
Breathe in for five seconds
1, 2, 3, 4, 5
Breathe out for five seconds
5, 4, 3, 2, 1

As I concentrate and breathe in for five seconds with each breath,
I rise into who I am becoming.

*As I concentrate and breathe
out for five seconds,
I settle into who I am.*

*Today I sit in silence
focusing on the rising and
falling of my chest,*

with each breath,

releasing

*emotional ties,
attachments,
and anything that does not
serve me,
becoming
more aware of myself.*

I am patient.

I take my time.

I let go.

I release.

I ask for help.

I breathe.

*I was given permission to live
out loud the moment
God
blew breath into me.
When I fell by the wayside it
was my elders who reminded me
of who granted me that
permission and to remember
who
I am
and to
Live.*

I use my breath to create space and cultivate ease within. With each intentional breath, my mind and body settle more and more

in

to

itself.

When I arrive at a place that I thought I was ready for and it turns out to be a huge mess, I instantly remember that I don't know what God, my source, my guiding light may be doing at the moment with me,
so I slow down,
take a breath,
and navigate the mess with patience, understanding, compassion, and the wisdom bestowed upon me remembering,
that sometimes,
I am
that mess.

Grace.

*As I go into today, I remind myself that all challenges are an opportunity for growth.
My patience and boundaries will be tested, and I may feel unbalanced when that happens I will then pause, breathe, and remember*

who
I am

and

who I am,
welcomes a challenge.

My heart is open and ready to absorb the affirmative energy of the universe so I can experience more.

*I catalog my experiences in a journal to promote continuous growth in my journey,
it allows me to visualize how far I have come,
and it is a gentle reminder of how far I still must go.*

*I honor my present by being
content where
I am.
I have ceased playing
tug-of-war
with the
moments I had stolen in my
past
versus
the anxiety of the 'what-ifs' of
my future.*

The past is the past, I released it so I can now live fully in the promise of God, uncovering what he had placed in my heart before I was introduced to my momma's womb.

*I receive each interaction
with an open heart and mind
in return
extending the gifts of grace
and compassion.*

It is the small things...it is the invisible things...the things I was born with...the things I sometimes choose to look beyond to find instead of looking within.

Those things are what makes me special, and it is not my job to explain them, it is my job to nurture them-

the gifts, I was given.

*As I stay grounded in my truth, I am calm, and that calmness allows me to settle gradually into my soul, my mind, my heart, and my body exploring
what is, right now at this very moment.
The past cannot be changed, and the future has not yet arrived.
As I heal, the tension I hold dissolves. As it dissolves new energy is created and that energy directs me to succumb to my vulnerabilities, building upon them, turning them into strengths to conquer*

what I once feared.

My energy is flowing, and I am using its force to heal my mind, heart, body, and soul.

*I direct and look over the
energy that flows in and through
me... I am the custodian of that
energy.
That is where my focus lies.
The energy I build upon and
the energy I guard even from my
own ego.*

Some people will refuse to know me pass who they expect me to be and become. I do not get bewildered because of that, I let them live in their head as I become my future.

*I allow myself the same
fresh start
as a new morning.*

*In rest,
I listen to my mind, heart, body, and soul, they speak to me through vibrational cues sent from the universe to care for me and protect me.*

As I meditate my physical, emotional, mental, and spiritual bodies are pleasingly combined.

As I move my body through moving meditation, dance, working out, or walking, I move my body based on subtle hints the spirit gives me to release fluid movement. I move my body effortlessly releasing tension. The feeling of release makes me smile letting go of others' thoughts and reminding myself that my thoughts are the only ones that matter. Moving my body energizes my mind, body, heart, and soul aligning them with Spirit.

I walk through life with fluidity and grace as I explore my creativity and tune into my own rhythm.

I am physically and mentally free of stress.

Moving my body is comforting for me.
Moving my body takes me through past, present, and future thoughts.
As I move my body through those thoughts, I am reminded that just like I am only responsible for my body I am only responsible for minding my own thoughts and not the words or thoughts of others.
I move and let go with each breath, settling deeper into myself breathing and letting go, feeling at ease and beautiful in my being as I glow from the inside out.

I bring awareness to both the feminine and masculine energy flowing through my body to deepen my life's Experiences.

I am committed to doing less so I can feel more.

I embrace how I feel with patience and understanding so I can move freely through each moment with intention and ease.

*As I honor my body,
I give thanks to the element of
water for it cleanses me,
hydrates me,
lubricates me,
and refreshes me when needed.*

Water is life.
Water has healing and transformational properties and if we let it, it will balance the body and create physical harmony.
Water symbolizes rebirth, spiritual cleansing, and salvation.

I am present in my body.

*I rise
with renewed energy
and a
positive attitude.*

*I focus on myself.
Not how I look but how my mind, body, and heart feel in this present moment of alignment, giving myself grace and being thankful for my many blessings at this very moment.
I appreciate these moments and all that they bring me.*

*I am here in this moment at this very second letting go figuratively and literally of what I am holding onto that is keeping me from fully welcoming my purpose.
I with open hands, free of baggage, am grounding myself where planted.
Right here,
right now
in my purpose.*

*I bring harmony into the landscape of my mind, with a fresh and renewed perspective of ease,
releasing the words busy and stress.*

I bring into existence a new day with reawakened energy.

I rest in my awareness as I navigate difficult emotions with greater ease and acceptance. In doing this it feels natural to let go of what does not serve me creating space for what does.

I pause...realigning myself in my purpose, no longer seeking answers from my past resting in the comfort of deep reflection knowing it was my past that led me to dwell deep within and rediscover my purpose.

*I am forever learning,
I am teachable,
trainable,
and
coachable.
I am humble.*

Healing is a personal intimate act, where I became lonely until I found myself.

*I do not want to be strong
enough to handle a situation,
I want to be vulnerable
enough to work through it.*

I am patient, I take my time, and I surrender my mind to rest commanding stillness to enter in so I can be able to think clearly and to advance carefully and gradually throughout the day.

When I become full of nervous energy I pause and ground, I draw calming energy from the earth calming the nervous energy and reminding me of the peace within.

*I am connecting with the earth,
feeling its support,
and
using its power of vibration to strengthen me.*

As I evolve, I let go of all attachments no longer averting from the truth in fear of disconnecting from the world.

This journey I am on leads me to grow, opening a door to healing, and returning me to what God has purposed in me.

I give time and attention to a daily action that keeps me advancing in a forward motion. I am intentionally living in each moment for my destiny is approaching.

May I have clarity of mind
May I speak with intention
May my thoughts and actions
mirror the peace within my soul
May my body be free of any
discomfort
May my heart overflow with
pure joy
and may I always go with the
direction of the animated force
within me
Making space to embrace my
passion
Leaving me free to live out my
purpose

I give myself the gift of being fully present in my mind and body as I sit in the spirit.

I will maximize my unique set of gifts by taking responsibility for gaining the knowledge and trust needed to trust myself completely with them.

*I am open to love
I give love
Doors are opening on behalf of
Love
for
me.*

*I am present in my body.
I am connecting with my body.*

Being present and connecting with my body allows me to tune in to the areas where extra love is needed in my body.

*Just as the lotus reblooms
we do.
Every morning we open our
eyes we get another chance to
rise with the sun,
another chance at life.*

*I extend grace to my body as I grow into each day with compassion and understanding.
I rise,
I radiate,
I lead with a clear mind.*

I meditate in Grace for Grace. In the presence of Grace is the absence of struggle, discontent, tension, and uncertainty because it is with grace I make the choice to let go and just be.

I move through my journey with grace and love discovering who I have always been. No longer letting my spirit hunger for the synchronicity of love, patience, and understanding in my mind, heart, body, and soul.

I lean with ease into uncomfortable situations knowing for sure that this too shall pass.

Clarity of mind paired with exercising patience leads me to be slow to act and gentle with movement.

The love I have for myself grows as I forgive myself for the events I settled for in the past.

*Man creates things to be the same.
Our Creator creates things to be unique.
I remember this when I am walking in my purpose, I remember that I am a masterpiece created to master peace.*

Interruptions can be helpful.

They initiate a pause.

Pause is where I practice stillness.

In stillness is where my thoughts are easy to perceive.

Pause.

Compassion is not a mystery, it is an act of kindness that I should always exhibit to all that I encounter. Displaying compassion lets everyone that I encounter know that they have a soft place to land in me.

I go deeper within me to heal. I am grounded and I am willing to explore even when it gets tense. I stay there in the intensity, in the face of vulnerability, releasing it into the universe to move on.

In being intentional about my healing, I am monitoring my thoughts, and being intentional about my responses.

I am finding balance in my life by not overexerting myself and resting when needed.

*I am smart enough to know
what I do not know
and
humble enough to ask for
help.*

What happened to me in the past did not weaken my present, acknowledging and sharing it strengthened my future.

I respect and honor all my relationships, from all of them I gained lessons, and through those lessons, my awareness increased.

I listen
I process
I respond
I do not react

I am cultivating patience and compassion within myself so I can extend and exercise patience and compassion to others.

I am creating space for continuous growth, joy, and love for myself knowing I did my best.

I have released the confines of the deep-rooted tension that kept my mind conditioned. The blockages are gone I am free to be me.

I made one small change, then another, then another, and then there was a shift.

I shift.

The extraordinary is now restored.
I am living in my power.

*I am walking in my power.
I am 100% attentive to each step.*

The clarity of my mind connects me to a deeper sense of self.
Joy
Success
Abundance
Creativity
Connection
I can complete everything I start.
In me, I have everything I need, and abundance is mine.

I sit with the reality of truth in every unfolding moment as it nourishes my mind, body, heart, and soul.

I am light,
I am refreshed,
I am renewed,
I am restored.

My patience flows into His divine timing.

I have unpacked all that was weighing me down. I now move forward experiencing all that this journey has to offer.

Truth is my resting place, truth is where my healing began, truth is the nourishment, my mind, body, heart, and soul need. I no longer hide from the truth I rise in the truth.

I commit to living a life of integrity and excellence so that I can increase in growth.

Love.
Charity.
Support.
Connection.

Like words, thoughts come and go. I let them flow, I take in the good and let go of the bad.

My ancestors carried me through their life pouring into me healing, love, hope, faith, joy, and wisdom. In their death, I carry what they have poured into me to share with others. That is where my power comes from.

I thank my ancestors for trusting me with the wealth that was poured into me.

I AM

I have learned the same way we welcome and usher life in, is the same way we should welcome death and usher death out, with compassion, empathy, and love.

In prayer, I connect with the truth.
I don't hunger for answers to be revealed because I know they will be revealed in His perfect timing.

Reshaping my mind and heart to receive an abundance of new blessings.

There is healing flowing through every cell in my body. I am well.

I am intentional about each endeavor I explore, and I will reign.

*I am grateful for my failures.
My failures are a chance to learn.
My failures are a sign for me to pause and collect my thoughts.
My failures give me another chance to do my best.
My failures are a chance to shower myself with grace, forgiveness, compassion, and love.*

And when I fail, in my understanding of self, I know that failure is a hint to slow down, gather my thoughts, and know that I am supposed to be here, right in this moment of failure, being patient, until that failure catapults me into something magnificent.

My mind is open to receiving the lessons failure bestows upon me.

I am creating the life I dreamed of by aligning vibrationally with who I AM.

I value my journey, I am happy, healthy, and healing.

*I know failure and success
go
hand in hand.
In knowing that
I
will
keep moving forward.*

*I create more life by saying "yes"
to new experiences and adventures.*

*I move through my purpose
not only
recognizing
but
understanding that the
blessing
is in the
release.*

*I am discovering
and
evolving
into the person the
universe
has been waiting for.*

Dear Ground,

Thank you for being there after every fall, for having my back, and for encouraging me to come back to my center physically, spiritually, and mentally. Thank you for letting me feel you so I could rise back up into my crown, giving me the space I needed so I can focus and write my next chapter in life.

Thank you I will always need you.

Growth inspires change and change is hard but beautiful.

My goal- Stay Beautiful

*I am growing, maturing, and changing.
Joyfully
witnessing the
evidence of life, in me.*

*I am connected to and
through God
My body is relaxed
my heart is open
my mind is clear
my soul is awake
I am connected.
I am well
I am good
I am one with who I am*

Patience requires me to pause and be still.
Patience brings divine connection.
Patience brings balance.
I rest in patience.

I connect to my deepest emotions, embracing the quietness of my mind, releasing tension while tapping into my full potential.

I let go of deep physical and mental stress by introducing mindfulness into my daily regimen.

I am deliberate and intentional about my being.

*I will never let my
past
or
future
steal my
present.*

I have the courage to say no.
I have the courage to speak up.
I have the courage to stay.
I have the courage to walk away.
I have the courage to be uncomfortable.
It takes courage to have courage.

*I make the
choice
to
drive change.*

*Opportunities are given to me
to strengthen and humble me,
so
I will not
forget
who
I am.*

I am intentional.
I set intentions every day and as I witness them, I appreciate them even more.
I take responsibility for each intention I set knowing I have true clarity of my mind and I am taking charge of my life.
I walk in my intentions, and I own them.

I pause,

put my best foot forward and come through.

*I stay centered as I am
moving in my own lane.
I move through life with
consistency and confidence
accomplishing
goal
after
goal
when distractions arise,
I know they are only
distractions,
so I just keep moving through.*

As a queen, I am not scared to make a move even if I am not aware of the outcome. I strategize with patience as I take action to win and not only in that moment but in life. I surround myself with experts that counsel me when it is needed, making sure the decisions I make are not predictable as I master the art of being gracefully deliberate while recognizing and learning from tactics used by my opponents.

*I have the courage to follow my dreams,
the heart to inspire others,
and the harmony to cooperate.*

*I release resistance,
leaving my mind and body to
freely think without reservation
and
move without hesitance.*

I break free of the chains of excuses.
My reasons to live in my purpose outweigh any excuse I tell myself not to follow His Will.

*When my vision gets blurry,
and my understanding is
limited
I will
trust the source,
my guiding light,
my God
to
lead me through.*

*By owning my emotions,
I took the first step toward
gaining control over my fears.
Courage, confidence, and
vulnerability gave me the
strength to overcome my fears
and start my healing process.*

*I pull up,
show up,
take a seat at the table,
and show initiative.*

Opportunities present their selves when I show up.

I learned how to trust my joy and stopped pushing it away.

Life is about understanding, forgiveness, learning, and loving.
Once that is understood that is when forgiving and being grateful for everything and everyone comes naturally...with boundaries.

*By accepting my reality,
I no longer live in my past
and
I can reflect upon my life
without bitterness, regret,
anger, and pain,
I can focus on the present,
and start the process I need to
evolve into a better me for my
future.*

Healing.

*With my ancestors,
a wing and a prayer
that's how I flow.*

*Part of the journey is healing from past wounds.
In healing...I rest.*

*I never know when an opportunity will present itself.
I will get ready so I will be ready when the opportunity presents itself.
The time is always now.*

*I stopped getting caught up in the word fail.
F.A.I.L.
means
First Attempt In Learning
Failing is a part of the learning process and what I realize is that in those moments of failure are teachable moments where I can evaluate the process and make it better.*

*I am grateful for learning how
to find joy in simplicity,
finding strength in times of
weakness,
having faith among the
faithless,
and loving beyond measure.*

*I find freedom in pausing,
it gives me a sense of ease
allowing me to dwell in the
knowledge that pausing is
natural,
it is a cure for stress and/or
anxiety.
Pausing silences the
interruptions allowing me to
rest, release, and ultimately
restore so that I can move
forward and beyond.*

I summon my confidence in each waking moment.

*I ask no one to forgive my bluntness,
for I am walking in confidence with what I was promised...
my purpose.*

My womanhood belongs to me what I choose to do with it is my right.

It is not what I am supposed to do.
It is what I want to do.
I will not let society define my life.
I will define it.

Life is short and tomorrow is not promised so
I
will
LIVE
in
each
moment.

Favor smiles upon me.

*In authenticity alignment happens.
People and opportunities will come,
and some will go.
I will let them.
In alignment, the universe opens my eyes to change, I will take heed and embrace change.*

I learned to give love to the smallest, quietest of gestures...they deserve love too.

*I am in a state of unlearning,
I now can clearly look beyond
my own limitations and look
inward toward my God-given
purpose in life.*

I ask for forgiveness

*I open my heart to receive
God's mercy*

I move forward with life

Love.
Love is an action verb.
Love is a decision that one chooses to make.
Love is a journey.

With patience comes wisdom. Sacrifice now, reap rewards later.

Prepare a place where your body, mind, heart, and soul can become one and that is when your inner peace will prevail.

*I surrender all that is around me so I can have peace within.
I don't look at surrendering as giving up, surrendering to me means letting go and having the understanding that some things are out of my control.*

The results I obtain will flow directly from my inner thoughts and the work I put in.

*I stop letting people put their idea of sexy in my head.
Sexy is the confidence I glow in,
I stand out in, the walk I slay in,
that sparkle in my eyes,
that authority in my voice,
that knowledge that I kick.
The way I express myself when silent.
It's an attitude.
Sexy is what I want it to be.*

*I am the architect of my life;
I build its foundation and
choose its contents.*

Out
of
the
place
of
Almost.

*Every day I change,
sometimes in stillness,
sometimes in chaos,
sometimes with no warning,
sometimes without a plan.*

Break-ups are hard, they hurt, and although the person may still be here physically I grieve. I will miss the person but in understanding everyone's growth is different and we all take different paths, it is with that understanding, that my grief dissipates and life goes on.

I forgive those who have harmed me in my past and peacefully detach from them.

Excuses are what I once made up when I was scared to face the reality of the decisions I made. I make no more excuses.

In my sorrow, comfort will come to find me giving me a safe place to land.

In that safe place is where I remember that in my grief and anger, God will lift me up in his strength and power so I can rest in His Will.

*I am healing my relationship with myself.
Healing is transformational.*

In healing, I learned I had to have compassion for myself to comfort and care for myself instead of blaming myself for things I had no control over. In doing that I was able to increase a sense of connection to help others honestly without judgment and criticism.

I am the embodiment of the information I choose to accept and act upon.

To change my circumstances, I changed my thinking and subsequent actions.

Today I turn my attention inward to clear the sound of chaos and focus on myself...gracing myself with my presence...clearing all obstacles...sitting with my thoughts as I let some thoughts stay and internally digest what is needed and let some thoughts go, having compassion for what does not belong, here at this moment and thereafter...then... giving thanks to who I am.

*With ease,
I surrender into who I am
becoming not void of suffering
but with the awareness of his
will in me. I surrender,
I let go,
I melt
and I align with who
I am
becoming.*

In understanding that I have yet to accomplish more of the experiences I set out to do, I understand I will have the company of unwelcome surprises.

In understanding that, I will be gentle with myself understanding that the unwelcomed surprises should not make me anxious but patient, and those surprises although unwelcomed I will use them as learning experiences.

God.
May you search my mind,
heart, body, and spirit.
May you replenish, restore,
and heal me of what is needed
to move forward in the fulfilling
life that I am purposed to live.
In your search may you fill
any empty holes with grace,
patience, and love and dispel all
unpleasantries you find.
May you lead me to the light
opening a space for me to
embrace the in-between period
where I will patiently wait and
graciously prepare to walk in
my purpose.

EMBODYING MY I AM

I gave up on waiting for certainty and started trusting the unfolding of the process.

*Life is short so I have fun
breaking the rules,
I always forgive quickly,
I kiss slowly,
I truly love,
I hug tightly,
I laugh uncontrollably and
loud
and I will never regret
anything that made me smile.*

I challenge myself to take responsibility for myself and my actions in times of weakness and in times of strength.

*As my soul heals,
my mind expands,
my heart opens,
my body decompresses
enabling me to enjoy my
presence in each moment;
in me, his spirit reigns.*

My healing began through journaling, music, and others' kindness, understanding, compassion, and empathy toward me.

In return, I share my gifts with the world including my kindness, understanding, compassion, and empathy towards others- mass enlightenment.

I am willing to step outside of my comfort zone to accomplish the goals I set for myself.

*I go into this next phase of life with an abundance of joy welcoming the unexpected surprises
as they
sharpen my awareness and awaken me to fully enjoy this journey committing fully to me.*

*As I water myself with
self-affirmations of
faith,
hope,
love,
confidence,
and grace
I always remember to add a
generous amount of
self-reflection for continued
growth.*

*I love hard,
forgive often,
smile contagiously,
practice compassion,
invest wisely,
give generously,
get upset,
get over it.
I feel through it,
heal through it,
and
grow through it.*

*I decided to love myself.
I became the embodiment of
what I am purposed to be and
not what they said I would be.
I took my fears and turned
them into challenges, as I rose
and took comfort in my faults
and mistakes by looking at them
as welcomed opportunities.*

*I never gave up or gave in.
I chose myself.*

*One key to remembering who
I am in a room full of chaos is
not worrying about
what they say,
what everybody else is doing,
and
what nobody ain't doing.*

Today.
Come into my heart and spread patience for those who do not want to change for I know I was once them and I was given patience and understanding. Shower them with your love and grace and let them feel the Love of our God, Ancestors, and spiritual guides, and know that their love is sufficient and their guidance is here for our transformation.

Today, I come to you to ask you to lead me in grace as I welcome the ease, love, comfort, rest, and pleasure, I have been granted.

Help me surrender to the sweetness of ease, love, comfort, rest, and pleasure without feeling guilty because I once normalized and reveled in the opposite.

I prayed for this, I don't want to go back.

*I look up to the sky,
reach pass the clouds,
and say order my steps,
after that,
I step out on faith
and
I don't look back.*

I am deliberate with my goals, intentional about my choices, and selective of my environment.

*I release everything that does
not serve me
to make room for what does
so I can live a prosperous life
of more as I utilize and rest in
the power of now.*

Today as I continue on this journey through life, please give me the strength to keep commitments to myself, the patience to transform, and the audacity to stay the course.

May I serve my creator by walking in and sharing the gifts I was given.

Ancestors you gave me tools and secrets that I need to walk forth in these gifts that I was given and may I present them well and in decent order.

Ancestors you groomed me in the way of giving me subtle hints so that I can graciously serve and for that I thank you.

I ask for the confidence to trust myself to make it happen.

I ask for the courage to walk and be a representation of the gifts as I move through life.

I AM a deliverer of the gifts I

was given, a creation of the creator, a blessing from and to my bloodline.
I AM

Trust me with being a good steward of the currency that flows in and through me so that I can keep multiplying that currency to give unto others freely as they have given to me.

Currency is unlimited and it is constantly flowing.

*I find calmness in releasing,
my heart is ready and willing to receive favor,
I am awakened,
and
I stand firm, supported by the universe as I am guided by my creator, and held by my ancestors.
Not anxious about what might occur after the release just patient and here for what is next.*

As I go about this life please protect me from my enemies and myself, bless me with your peace grace, and love.

Bless me with your forgiveness, compassion, and empathy.

As I walk through this life I honor the journey and the lessons I have learned.

*I journey in awe of you and with you knowing that **I AM** one of many and I humbly ask you to keep me safe in your arms.*

*Guide me in who I am so I can be my best in my becoming.
Walk before and clear the way.
Walk before me creating steps to the next level.
Walk before me and lift me up over unforeseen obstacles.
Walk before me and slow me down if need be and give me a sign to be patient.*

If you ever feel my idleness is not of rest but of laziness heal whatever it is that has me idle.

I open my hands and heart to receive the goodness that life bestowed upon me.

I stand tall with my back straight and my head high, rising into my crown, understanding this is my God-given right as I was created to receive good things.

Spirit, give me the discernment to hear with the intent of listening so I can understand the messages I am receiving.

*The next pages in this book are dedicated to you.
It is Space for you to write Affirmations, Notes to Self, and Prayers.*

I AM...

I AM...

Dear Me,

Dear Me,

Today I Feel...

Today I Feel...

What signs are my body giving me today?

What signs are my body giving me today?

What is God trying to tell me?

What is God trying to tell me?

What do I need to release?

What do I need to release?

Kishna Marie is an author who resides in Vail, AZ. Kishna uses her love of writing as a healing agent to soothe the inner wounds of early childhood trauma and empowers others to do the same by looking within their selves and using the hurt, pain, and suffering as tools to strengthen their minds, hearts, bodies, and souls. Kishna is a 200YTT practitioner and enjoys journaling, the outdoors, gardening, dancing, food, and traveling.

Other Works by Kishna Marie
Healing Will Have You *Trippin'*...I HEAL AS I WRITE

www.ingramcontent.com/pod-product-compliance
Lightning Source LLC
Chambersburg PA
CBHW072152100526
44589CB00015B/2203